The Great British Baking Cookbook

30 Traditional Baking Recipes for Bakers of All Abilities

By

Martha Stephenson

License Notes

No part of this Book can be reproduced in any form or by any means including print, electronic, scanning or photocopying unless prior permission is granted by the author.

All ideas, suggestions and guidelines mentioned here are written for informative purposes. While the author has taken every possible step to ensure accuracy, all readers are advised to follow information at their own risk. The author cannot be held responsible for personal and/or commercial damages in case of misinterpreting and misunderstanding any part of this Book

Table of Contents

Introduction

We have collected 30 mouth-watering British bakes, made the good, old-fashioned way! If you're looking to improve your pastry-making skills, or to be able to make that perfect fruit cake for Christmas, then this is the book for you. Arm yourself with a couple of dozen eggs, a sack of flour, a whole heap of sugar, and possibly even your own cow to provide you with butter, and get to work on these crowd-pleasing bakes. Oh, and of course, if you really want to do things the traditional British way, you'll have to serve everything with a freshly brewed cup of tea. Join me now on a historical journey through the lengths and breadths of Great Britain and give your tastebuds and those of your family and friends a moist, buttery, and sweet treat!

Iced Bakewell Tart

No British baking book would be complete without that tried and tested classic, the Bakewell tart. Hailing from Northern England, this sweet raspberry and almond flavoured tart has really stood the test of time. Traditionally, it's not iced, but it just adds that extra something, so we've included an iced version for you here.

Serves: 10

Preparation time: 90 minutes

Ingredients:

- 11 1/2 oz. icing sugar
- 11 oz. butter
- 9 oz. jam sugar
- 8 oz. plain flour
- 7 oz. raspberries

- 5 ½ oz. caster sugar
- 5 ½ oz. ground almonds
- 3 cups rice (or baking balls)
- 2 eggs
- 2 teaspoons almond extract
- ½ teaspoon pink food colouring

Serving suggestion:

If you have extra raspberry jam, spoon an extra dollop onto your slice and enjoy.

1) In a saucepan, begin to heat the raspberries. Crush them using a masher and then add in the jam sugar. Boil for 4 minutes and then leave aside to cool and set a little.

2) Pour the plain flour into a bowl and crumb in half of the butter, ensuring that it was chilled. Once it resembles breadcrumbs, add in 1 oz. icing sugar.

3) Beat one of the eggs and add it into the dough mix, along with 2 tablespoons of water. Combine everything well together to form a dough.

4) Roll the dough out to just under an inch thickness and line a round tart pan with it. Then, refrigerate for 30 minutes.

5) Preheat the oven to 390°F.

6) Place a sheet of greaseproof paper into the tart tin on top of the pastry. Pour in the rice or baking balls and bake for 15

minutes. Remove the paper and leave just the pastry to cook for a further 5 minutes.

7) Reduce the oven temperature to 350°F.

8) Cream together the remaining butter and caster sugar. Add the second egg, one teaspoon of the almond extract and the ground almonds and mix well together.

9) Spread 4-6 tablespoons of the raspberry jam along the bottom of the pastry shell. Then, spoon the almond mixture on top evenly. Bake for 25-30 minutes until golden brown and an inserted skewer comes out clean.

10) To make the icing, sift the ice sugar and stir in the second teaspoon of almond extract and 3 tablespoons of water. Take 3 tablespoons of the icing aside and add the link food colouring into this part.

11) When the tart is completely cooled, spread the white icing smoothly over the top. Then, pipe on the pink icing in lines. Take a cocktail stick and drag it through the icing in lines at a 90° angle to create a 'feather' effect.

Tips: If you are looking to build up your baking repertoire, we suggest investing in some baking balls and a piping bag, as this recipe calls for. These are tools that will come in handy again and again.

A true, traditional Bakewell tart does not have icing, so feel free to make your life a little easier and skip the icing.

Jaffa Cakes

As one of Britain's best-loved snacks, the Jaffa cake has become a staple in pantries and lunch boxes alike. For those unfamiliar, these 'biscuits' have a spongy bottom layer topped with orange jelly and then dark chocolate. The real question though, is it a cake, or is it a biscuit? This has been puzzling Jaffa cake lovers for centuries. I'll let you make your own mind up once you've tried out this recipe.

Makes: 12

Preparation time: 90 minutes

Ingredients:

- 6 ¼ oz. dark chocolate
- 4 ¾ oz. orange jello blocks
- 1 small orange
- 1 egg
- 1 oz. caster sugar
- 1 oz. self-raising flour
- Butter or oil for greasing

Serving suggestion:

If you want to jazz this up into a real dessert, you could candy or caramelise segments leftover from the orange and serve the Jaffa Cakes along with those and form fresh whipped cream.

1) In a bowl, dissolve the orange jello in 5 fl oz. of boiling water. Grate the orange zest in too and stir well. Refrigerate for at least an hour, until set.

2) Preheat oven to 350°F. Grease a cupcake tray.

3) Whisk together the sugar and egg until light and fluffy. Then, fold in the flour.

4) Fill in each hole of the tin to about ¾ full and ensure that the tops are smoothed. Bake for 7-9 minutes, until well risen and springy.

5) Melt the chocolate in a heatproof bowl over a pan of simmering water.

6) Turn out the jelly and cut a disc for each cake. Make sure that it's small enough that when placed in the centre, there is at least ½ an inch to spare around the edges.

7) Place an orange disc in the centre of each mini sponge.

8) Spoon the chocolate to cover the top of each sponge. To create the traditional pattern, use the prongs of a fork to draw some lines in the centre, over where the jelly was.

Tips: This is only a small amount of cake batter, so using a hand mixer rather than an electric one would probably work better. An electric one may end up spraying!

This recipe obviously creates a more 'cake-y' version than the store bought option. If you want a harder, more biscuit-y base like the ones from the store, then leave them for a few days in a container that's not quite airtight.

Chelsea Buns

The Chelsea bun has a long history in the contented stomachs of happy Brits, young and old alike. Dating back to at least the mid 1800's, but likely earlier, these buns were once described as "roving vagrant buns", due to their place as a staple on the trays of cake and pie vendors wandering the streets of London. Try your hand at these and enjoy the childish thrill of these sweet and sticky little treats.

Makes: 10-12

Preparation time: 90 minutes

Ingredients:

- 30 oz. plain flour
- 7 oz. butter
- 4 oz. caster sugar
- 3 ½ oz. raisins
- 3 eggs
- 2 teaspoons cinnamon
- 1 ¾ oz. brown sugar
- 1 3/4 fl oz. milk
- 1 lemon
- ¾ oz. yeast
- ½ teaspoon ground nutmeg

Serving suggestion:

Thinking back to the humble beginnings of these buns on the poor streets of London, these would've been accompanied by none other than the Great a British 'cuppa'.

1) Warm 1 ¼ fl oz. of the milk. Then, mix it with 3 ½ oz. of the plain flour, ¾ oz. of the caster sugar and the yeast. Keep at a temperature of roughly 85°F and allow it to stand until it has frothed and fallen in on itself again.

2) Take 2 ¾ oz. of the butter and allow it to soften. Then, sift together the remaining flour and the nutmeg. Rub in the softened butter until the mixture resembles breadcrumbs.

3) Into the yeast mix, whisk in most of the caster sugar, leaving about ½ oz. spare, 2 eggs and the zest of the lemon. Then, add this into the breadcrumbs and combine together to create a dough.

4) Cover the dough with a towel and leave to stand for an hour. Then, re-knead the dough, knocking out the air and getting the dough back down to its original size.

5) Roll the dough out into a rectangle of about ¼ inch in height, with straight edges and sharp corners.

6) Melt 1 ¾ oz. of butter and brush it all over the surface of the dough. Then, sprinkle on evenly the cinnamon, brown sugar and raisins.

7) Using the longer side of the rectangle, tightly roll the dough over and over into a tube. Then, cut along the tube even 1 ½ inches to create the individual buns.

8) Shape each bun into a square and place on a lined baking tray.

9) Beat the last egg with a little melted butter and then brush this over the buns as a glaze.

10) Place the buns into uniform rows and leave to rise for a further 30 minutes.

11) Preheat the oven to 410°F.

12) Bake for 20-25 minutes, until risen and golden brown.

13) Dissolve the last remaining caster sugar in the rest of the milk and then brush this over the buns.

Tips: The dough will work best if it's not sticky. Therefore, if necessary, add extra flour when combining the ingredients to create a firmer dough.

Try to roll as tightly as possible during the tube process to create buns that will certainly stick together.

Jam Tarts

There is an old English children's rhyme that says that 'the queen of hearts made some tarts'. Then 'the knave of hearts stole those tarts'! Well, if her tarts were perfect individual little jam tarts, then we certainly don't blame that naughty knave! When making your own versions, keep your eyes out for little thieves! Or, you could be nice and share, but we're not sure you'll want to!

Makes: 12

Preparation time: 75 minutes

Ingredients:

- 12 oz. plain flour
- 6 oz. butter
- 3 tablespoons lemon juice
- 3 teaspoons caster sugar
- 1 ½ cups jam sugar
- 1 cup strawberries
- 1 cup blackberries
- 1 cup orange segments
- Pinch of salt

Serving suggestion:

Unlike a lot of baked goods, these are actually better cooled or even chilled! A major reason for this of course is that jam straight from the oven is actually the temperature of the surface of the sun!

1) Place each cup of fruit in a separate pan and add ½ a cup of jam sugar and a tablespoon of lemon juice. Mash or crush the fruit a little and leave to simmer for 10-15 minutes until the mixture becomes thick and syrupy. Try to mash the fruit as much as possible, as we need smooth jams for this recipe. Pass the jams through a sieve and use the back of a spoon to push through as much as possible. Leave all 3 in separate bowls and put to one side to cool.

2) Crumb together the flour, butter, caster sugar and a pinch of salt. Gradually add in up to 4 fl oz. of cool water to form a dough. Cling wrap the dough and leave it to chill for 30 minutes.

3) Preheat the oven to 350°F and grease a tart tray or two, however many you need for your 12 tarts.

4) Roll the dough out to about ¼ inch thickness and cut out 12 rounds for the tart bases. Place these in the greased trays and bake for 10 minutes.

5) After the 10 minutes, fill the bases with the jam, making 4 of each flavour. Fill it up to ¼ inch from the top of the tart case. Bake for an additional 10 minutes until all pastry is golden brown.

Tips: This recipe gives you 3 different flavours of jam, to mix it up a little. If you want to simplify, feel free to use just one flavour of jam, or even store-bought stuff.

If you have leftover dough from making the 12 rounds, then you can make some decoration to go on top. Cut out small hearts, circles, or squares and place them in the centres of the tarts, on top of the jam.

Figgy Pudding

Warning! – Figgy Pudding may not contain any actual figs (this one does though)! Whilst we probably now won't ever know the true reason why, it's thought that the word 'figgy' actually came from older puddings called 'fygeye'. Whatever the origins, modern figgy pudding is a dense and yummy fruit cake, traditionally served at Christmas, a real 'Winter warmer'.

Serves: 12

Preparation time: 90 minutes

Ingredients:

- 12 dried figs
- 3 eggs
- 2 cups breadcrumbs
- 2 teaspoons baking powder
- 1 ½ teaspoons cinnamon
- 1 ¼ cups plain flour
- 1 cup brown sugar
- 1 cup dried cranberries
- 1 cup dried apricots
- 1 teaspoon ginger
- ½ cup raisins
- ½ cup butter
- ½ cup spiced rum
- ½ teaspoon nutmeg
- ½ teaspoon cloves
- ¼ cup brandy
- Pinch of salt

Serving suggestion:

As you may realise during the cooking process, this is actually pretty close to traditional Christmas pudding! So, serve everyone up a slice after dinner and serve with brandy cream.

1) In a saucepan, gently simmer the figs, raisins, rums and brandy with ½ a cup of water. After 3 minutes, use a lighter to carefully light the mixture to burn off the alcohol for a minute or so. Then blow out the flame if it doesn't do it itself.

2) Mix together the flour, baking powder, slices and a pinch of salt.

3) Melt the butter and then mix into it the eggs, sugar, and breadcrumbs. Then, also stir in the mix of dry ingredients and the fig mixture.

4) Fold in the cranberries and apricots.

5) Grease a large pudding dish (a Bundt tin or Angel tin would be good too). Place it in a large, deep pan and pour water around the side until it comes halfway up the pudding tin.

6) Scoop the batter into the pudding tin and smooth it out. Cover with aluminium foil.

7) Bring the water to a simmer and then reduce the heat and allow the kidding to steam for another 2 hours. Check the after levels and keep it well topped up.

8) To serve, remove from the water bath and then flip over onto a plate.

Tips: This makes a lot of batter and requires large pans for the cooking. If easier, you can divide the mixture and make 2 smaller puddings.

This mixture is firmly fruit-based, but you can also add in some chopped nuts if you wish.

Fudge Tart

Anyone who spent their early years at a British public school will have some mixed memories about 'school dinners', some good, and some not so good. Always up there with the most delicious of memories though, is the school fudge tart. Sweet and topped with grated chocolate, it's easy to see why this is a favorite with the kids. They shouldn't be the ones having all the fun though, so here's a recipe for making your own version at home.

Serves: 8

Preparation time: 30 minutes + refrigeration

Ingredients:

- 9 ½ of oz. milk
- 8 oz. plain flour
- 5 ½ oz. margarine
- 3 oz. sugar
- 1 ½ oz. lard
- 1 teaspoon vanilla extract
- ½ oz. milk chocolate

Serving suggestion:

This is a pretty plain tart (although still super tasty). A yummy combination to add to it is fresh strawberries or banana.

1) Preheat the oven to 365° and grease a baking tin.

2) Sieve 6 oz. of the flour and then crumb together with the lard and 1 ½ oz. of margarine. Slowly add up to 1 ½ fl oz. of cold water to bind together into a dough.

3) Roll out the dough to ¼ inch thickness and line the baking tin with it. Bake for 15 minutes.

4) Meanwhile, bring half of the milk to the boil with the remaining margarine.

5) With the other half of the milk, beat in the remainder of the flour until it's formed a smooth paste and then add it to the boiling milk mixture. Add in the sugar and stir until everything is smooth and thickening.

6) Finally, add in the vanilla essence and then pour the fudge mix into the pastry base.

7) Refrigerate the tart and before serving, grate the milk chocolate on top.

Tips: If you have some available, using baking balls to 'blind bake' the pastry. You could also just place on top another sheet of greaseproof paper and then fill with some uncooked rice. This will stop the bottom of the pastry from rising and being uneven.

Most tarts are round, but if you want to be true to the 'school dinner' version, then you can actually bake it square or rectangular.

Peach Cobbler

If there's a time of year when Britain comes into its own, it's Winter. Whilst the winters are not usually majorly cold or snowy, they are grey, damp, and frosty. I know you're thinking that it's really no sounding too great, but actually this opens the door to a whole delicious range of hot baked desserts that just don't feel quite right unless it's miserable outside.

Serves: 6

Preparation time: 40 minutes

Ingredients:

- 8 ripe peaches
- 3 ½ oz. plain flour
- 3 ½ oz. butter
- 1 ¾ oz. caster sugar
- 1 ½ oz. brown sugar
- 1 ½ oz. pine nuts
- 1 teaspoon vanilla extract
- 1 lime
- 1 orange
- 1 inch fresh ginger
- Pinch of salt

Serving suggestion:

Nothing goes better with peaches than vanilla ice cream! Serve the cobbler piping hot and with a scoop of your best vanilla ice cream melting deliciously over the top.

1) Preheat the oven to 375°F.

2) Have and stone the peaches and then cut them into wedges.

3) In a casserole dish or earthenware baking dish, toss the peaches together with the vanilla extract and brown sugar. Grate on top the zests of the lime and the orange, and squeeze in the orange juice too. Cook for 10-15 minutes, until the peaches are starting to soften.

4) Blitz the pine nuts and add them into a bowl together with the flour, caster sugar and a pinch of salt. Add in the butter to create a breadcrumb mixture.

5) Add in roughly 2 tablespoons of water until the crumbs create a firm dough.

6) Once the peaches are out of the oven, pour on them about ½ a cup of water and stir everything again.

7) Dollop the dough in spoonfuls over the top of the peaches and then bake again for 20 minutes until golden brown.

Tips: If you don't have a food processor for the pine nuts, you can seal them firmly in a zip lock bag, making sure there's no trapped air, and then crush them with a rolling pin.

The topping is supposed to be uneven and the peaches should be poking through, so don't feel the need to smooth down your dollops.

Strawberry Shortcake

So, we hear a lot about Britain being cold and wintery, but there is also such a thing as the Great British summertime! Summer in England can really only mean one thing – strawberries! Strawberries really are some of the country's best produce. So, pick yourself up a punnet and set to work on the most summery of all desserts – fresh strawberry shortcake.

Serves: 6

Preparation time: 30 minutes

Ingredients:

- 8 ½ oz. plain flour
- 6 cups strawberries
- 6 tablespoons caster sugar
- 4 oz. butter
- 2 cups double cream
- 1 cup milk
- 1 teaspoon baking powder
- Pinch of salt
- Icing sugar to dust

Serving suggestion:

Since this is a summer recipe, allow the cakes to cool completely and refrigerate the strawberries and cream before assembling.

1) Preheat the oven to 400°F and line a baking sheet with greaseproof paper.

2) Mix together the flour, baking powder and a pinch of salt with 1 tablespoon of the caster sugar.

3) Rub the butter into the mixture and then pour in the milk. The batter should be fairly runny and easily droppable.

4) On the baking sheet, evenly drop the batter on in 6 dollops. Then, bake for 10-15 minutes, until golden brown.

5) Hull and halve the strawberries and mix in 3 tablespoons of caster sugar.

6) Whip the cream with the last 2 tablespoons of caster sugar to form soft peaks.

7) Once the cakes have cooled, halve them. Assembly by placing one half of the cake on the plate first. Then, top with some strawberries and a dollop of cream and finally sandwich the top layer of cake back on. Dust with icing sugar.

Tips: For a variation if you're more of a 'crunchy' person, you can switch out the cakes for shortbread biscuits.

To make a more professional looking product, place the strawberries on with care and then pipe the cream in the gaps between.

Battenberg

Not the most English-sounding name but certainly a cake of English origin is the Battenberg! Originating from the 1800's when the British monarchy was forming connections with the German house of Battenberg, this is also known as 'angel cake'. Almond-y, apricot-y and 2-toned – yes, this cake is a must-try.

Serves: 8-10

Preparation time: 30 minutes + refrigeration

Ingredients: For the marzipan:

- 6 ¼ oz. butter 15 ¾ oz. ground almonds
- 6 ¼ oz. caster sugar 9 ¾ oz. icing sugar
- 5 oz. self-raising flour 6 ¼ oz. caster sugar
- 3 eggs 2 eggs
- 4 cups fresh apricots 1 teaspoon vanilla extract
- 3 cups jam sugar ½ teaspoon orange juice
- 1 ½ oz. ground almonds
- 1/2 teaspoon baking powder
- 1/2 teaspoon vanilla extract
- ½ teaspoon almond extract
- 2/3 teaspoon pink food colouring
- ¼ cup lemon juice

Serving suggestion:

1) Between 24 and 48 hours in advance, you'll need to make the marzipan. In a bowl, mix together the ground almonds, icing sugar, and caster sugar. Make a well in the middle of the mix and pour in the eggs, vanilla extract, and orange juice. Cut the ingredients together. Flour a surface and begin to knead the dough. Once combined, shape into a ball, wrap in cling wrap and refrigerate until ready to use.

2) Preheat the oven to 350°F and line 2 long, rectangular baking tins of the same size with greaseproof paper.

3) Mix together the butter, caster sugar, flour, eggs, ground almonds, baking powder and vanilla and almond extracts to form a batter.

4) Divide the mixture in half and into one half, stir in the pink food colouring.

5) Pour the 2 batters into the 2 trays and bake for 25-30 minutes, until a skewer can be inserted and come out clean.

6) Meanwhile, we can make the apricot jam. Ensure that the apricots are peeled and pitted. Then, in a saucepan, bring them to a boil with the lemon juice, crushing the apricots as much as possible. Reduce down to a simmer and stir in the jam sugar until dissolved. Allow to thicken for 20-25 minutes and then remove from the heat. Strain the jam mixture so that you're left with a smooth mix.

7) Trim the edges of the two cakes so that you have even rectangles and then cut each in half. Trim the cakes up until you have 4 rectangles of equal size, 2 of each colour.

8) Roll out the marzipan into a large rectangle. The short side should be the same length as the long side of the cakes.

9) Brush the marzipan with apricot jam.

10) Place one cake of each colour side by side at one end of the marzipan, leaving about a 2 inch gap from the edge. You can brush the inside of the cakes with the apricot jam too, so that they stick together.

11) Brush the top of the cakes with the jam, and stick on the other 2 lengths, now with the pink on top of the yellow and vice versa, creating a checkerboard effect. Again, brush the inside edges with the jam to help them stick together.

12) Now, carefully take the marzipan and fold it over the cake, covering all of the sides. When you reach the 2 inch gap, press down and trim off any extra. Your cake should be a rectangle and all iced in marzipan.

Tips: If you're baking the 2 cakes at the same time, after 15 minutes, switch their positions in the oven so that they get an even chance to cook.

You can obviously use store-bought marzipan or jam, but we've included the recipes for fresh versions to give you the option of being that bit more impressive.

Lemon Drizzle Cake

If citrus is your thing then you're going to love lemon drizzle cake! A light and moist sponge with extra added lemony goodness through a 'drizzle' and candied peel. Nothing could be more lemony fresh.

Serves: 10

Preparation time: 90 minutes

Ingredients:

- 16 oz. caster sugar
- 8 oz. butter
- 8 oz. self-raising flour
- 4 eggs
- 2 lemons

Serving suggestion:

Here is a cake that screams summer. Really get your lemon on by serving this cake with a long, cool lemonade.

1) Preheat to 350°F and line a loaf tin with greaseproof paper.

2) Cut one lemon into slices and remove the peel. Bring the peels to boil in 2 ½ cups of water. When boiling, change for fresh water. Do this one more time so that they'll have been boiled 3 times. Drain the peels and remove from the heat. Bring to the boil 5 ¼ oz. of sugar with the same volume of water (roughly 2/3 of a cup). When simmering, add in the peels and stir until the pith has become translucent. Toss in a little extra sugar and then set aside to cool.

3) Cream together the butter and 8 oz. of the caster sugar. Add in the eggs one at a time and stir well after each addition.

4) Sift in the flour and then grate in the zest of 1 lemon. Stir everything well.

5) Pour the batter into the loaf tin and bake for 45-50 minutes until a skewer can be inserted and come out clean.

6) Juice the lemons and heat quickly with the remaining caster sugar and stir to create a smooth drizzle.

7) Prick the top of the cake all over with a skewer and pour the glaze on top. It will seep in and also pour down and around the sides. Top with the candied peel.

Tips: The candied peel can be made ahead of time. As long as it's stored in an airtight container, it'll keep for 2-3 weeks.

If you wait until the cake is cool for pouring on the drizzle, it's become more like a glaze.

Sticky Toffee Pudding

There's something so incredibly comforting about a rich, warm and sticky sauce-covered pudding. The best thing about these little charms are that they can be made in advance and heated up as you need. So, whip up a batch of seven and enjoy every night of the week!

Serves: 7

Preparation time: 75 minutes

Ingredients:

- 8 oz. Medjool dates
- 7 ½ fl oz. cream
- 6 ¼ oz. self-raising flour
- 6 ¼ oz. light muscovado sugar
- 5 oz. Demerara sugar
- 4 ¾ oz. butter
- 3 ¼ fl oz. milk
- 3 tablespoons black treacle
- 2 eggs
- 1 teaspoon vanilla extract
- 1 teaspoon baking powder

Serving suggestion:

This rich and warm pudding is perfectly complimented by some cold and creamy vanilla ice cream.

1) Preheat to 350°F and grease 7 mini pudding tins or ramekins. Place them in a deep baking dish.

2) Chop the dates up small and cover them with 6 fl oz. of boiling water. Leave for 30 minutes and then mash a little and stir in the vanilla extract.

3) Beat together 3 oz. of butter and sugar and then beat the eggs in one at a time.

4) Stir in 2 tablespoons of the treacle.

5) Fold in 1/3 of the flour and half of the milk. Repeat until all of the flour and milk is incorporated. Then, also stir in the baking powder.

6) Stir the dates into the batter and then divide the mixture evenly between the ramekins. Bake for 20-25 minutes, until risen and firm.

7) In a saucepan, heat the muscovado with the remaining butter and half of the cream. Bring to boil and then stir in the last tablespoon of treacle. Allow the mixture to boil for a further 3 minutes until it resembles a dark toffee. Take off of the heat and then stir in the remaining cream.

8) Turn out the puddings and pour the sauce over the top.

Tips: To make these puddings even more moist and sticky, you can sit the puddings in the sauce for up to a day beforehand. Pour half of the sauce into a baking tin and sit the puddings in it. Pour in the rest of the sauce and leave until ready to serve. Re-heat in the oven before serving.

For some texture, feel free to add some raisins or chopped nuts into either the cake batter or the toffee sauce.

Fondant Fancies

When creating miniature treats for an ever-so-English tea party, looking dainty and pretty is the order of the day. These adorable 'Alice in Wonderland'-esque little fondant fancies are the perfect bite sized treats for any sophisticated afternoon tea.

Makes: 25

Preparation time: 100 minutes + refrigeration time

Ingredients:

- 17 ½ white fondant icing, ready to roll
- 15 ½ oz. butter
- 10 oz. icing sugar
- 7 ½ oz. caster sugar
- 7 ½ oz. self-raising flour
- 7 oz. marzipan
- 4 eggs
- 3 teaspoons vanilla extract
- 2 oz. dark chocolate
- 2 tablespoons apricot jam
- Yellow food colouring
- Pink food colouring
- Green food colouring

Serving suggestion:

These would look adorable on an old-fashioned cake stand, accompanied by scones and mini sandwiches, and, of course, tea!

1) Preheat to 350°F and line a square baking tin with greaseproof paper.

2) Beat together 7 ½ oz. of butter with the caster sugar. Add the eggs one by one and beat well between each addition.

3) Fold in the flour and 2 teaspoons of vanilla extract.

4) Pour the batter into the baking tin and smooth the surface as well as you can. Bake for 40-45 minutes until a skewer can be inserted and come out clean.

5) Warm the jam and strain it to remove any lumps.

6) Brush the top of the cake with the jam.

7) Roll out the marzipan and place a layer along the top of the cake, sticking it down with the jam. Chill the cake for 10 minutes to allow it to stick together.

8) Beat together the remaining butter with the icing sugar and a teaspoon of vanilla extract to make buttercream icing.

9) Take the marzipan-topped cake and cut into 25 even squares. Cut 5 rows evenly spaced out one way, and then do the same the other way along the cake.

10) Spread a thin layer of the buttercream all around the 4 sides of each square, and then pipe a small blob in the centre on top. Chill for an hour.

11) In an electric mixer. Start to churn the fondant icing so that it begins to break up. Gradually, add in up to 3 ½ fl oz. cold water to bring it to a thin enough consistency for pouring.

12) Divide the icing into 3 separate bowls and add in the 3 types of food colouring drop by drop into each bowl until they reach your desired colour.

13) Stick a fork into the base of each cake to enable it to be dipped and coated in the icing, or so that the icing can be poured on top. Leave to set for 20 minutes.

14) Over a saucepan of simmering water, melt the dark chocolate, stirring regularly.

15) Pour the chocolate into a piping bag and use it to create a zig zag pattern over the top of each fancy.

Tips: In this recipe, for ease, we've used store-bought marzipan, apricot jam and fondant icing. If you want to be even more of a baking guru, feel free to make your own!

Traditionally, as these are petite little treats, the colouring is kept as soft, pastel colour, requiring only a small amount of colouring. Of course, feel free to go wild and create some rebellious boldly-coloured fancies too!

Butterfly Cakes

This recipe is perfect for a weekend baking session with the kids. The little cupcakes are incredibly easy to make, and, coupled with the fun of decoration and the thrill of adding wings(!) to them, this will be both exciting to make and delicious to chomp on.

Makes: 18

Preparation time: 50 minutes

Ingredients:

- 18 oz. icing sugar
- 18 oz. butter
- 8 oz. caster sugar
- 8 oz. self-raising flour
- 8 tablespoons strawberry jam
- 5 teaspoons vanilla extract
- 4 eggs
- 2 tablespoons milk

Serving suggestion:

Find some super-cute little cupcake cases and have a miniature tea party with the kids!

1) Preheat to 350°F and line muffin tins with 18 cupcake cases.

2) Whisk together 8 oz. of butter and the caster sugar until light and fluffy. Then, beat in the eggs one by one.

3) Sieve the flour and gently fold into the butter mixture.

4) Then, stir in 3 teaspoons of vanilla extract along with the milk and combine the mixture well.

5) Spoon the mixture into the cupcake cases, each should be ¾ of the way full.

6) Bake for 18-20 minutes, until risen and springy to the touch.

7) Meanwhile, beat the remaining 10 oz. of butter and then sift in the icing sugar. Pour in 2 teaspoons of vanilla extract and whisk until well-combined to make your buttercream icing.

8) Once the cakes have cooled slightly, carefully slice off the domed tops. Cut each dome in half, creating the 2 'wings'.

9) Ice the top of each cake with the buttercream.

10) Line with middle of the cake with ½ a tablespoon of strawberry jam and push the 2 'wings' into the buttercream, gently but firmly enough so that they stay standing. Dust with a little extra icing sugar if you wish.

Tips: If you want to make your own jam, it's super easy. Take a cup of strawberries and boil together with 2 cups of jam sugar, mashing the strawberries as you go.

To get a good dome on each little cake, fill the cases up pretty high to allow for rising and doming.

Parkin

Although on is one of Britain's lesser known traditional bakes, parkin is by no means lesser on flavour! Originating from the Northwest of England, parkin is a full-flavored treacle and ginger bake. There are variations from different towns in the area, but here we've opted for a classic sponge cake option.

Makes: 16 squares

Preparation time: 50 minutes

Ingredients:

- 8 ¾ oz. self-raising flour
- 7 oz. butter
- 7 oz. golden syrup
- 4 tablespoons milk
- 3 ½ oz. oatmeal
- 3 oz. treacle
- 3 oz. light brown sugar
- 1 egg
- 1 tablespoon ginger

Serving suggestion:

This cake can be pretty firm, so if you wanted to whip up a quick toffee sauce, that would complement the parkin perfectly.

1) Preheat to 320°F and grease a square baking tin.

2) Beat together the egg and milk.

3) In a pan, melt together the butter, golden syrup, treacle, and sugar until all dissolved.

4) Into the syrup mix, fold in the flour, oatmeal, and ginger and then also pour in the egg and milk.

5) Pour the batter into the baking tin and bake for 45-60 minutes, until the cake is firm and a crust had formed on the top.

6) Cut into 16 equally-sized squares and serve.

Tips: This cake gets more moist with time. If you can leave it for 2-3 days before eating, then you'll notice a difference. It'll keep for up to 2 weeks.

Obviously, back in the day, many spices were not readily available. Today, however, we're fortunate enough to have an abundance! Feel free to experiment with adding nutmeg, cinnamon or allspice.

Eccles Cakes

Named after their birthplace, Eccles, in Northwest England, these individual little pastries are a true British tradition. For some reason, though, these harmless treats were historically blamed for starting many a house fire! We don't think that something so delicious could do something so destructive, but we of course advise caution!

Makes: 8

Preparation time: 90 minutes + refrigeration time

Ingredients:

- 12 ¼ oz. plain flour
- 9 ¾ oz. butter
- 4 sugar cubes
- 3 ½ oz. muscovado sugar
- 7 oz. raisins
- 1 lemon
- 1 orange
- 1 egg
- 1 teaspoon cinnamon
- 1 teaspoon ginger
- 1 teaspoon allspice

Serving suggestion:

Strange though it may sound, the citrus and fruit filling of these cakes means that they go very well with some strong British cheese, such as a Lancashire or mature cheddar.

1) Take 8 ¾ oz. of the butter and dice up small. Place in the freezer to go very hard.

2) Then, pulse half of this butter together with the flour to create a breadcrumb-like mixture.

3) Zest and juice the lemon. Set the zest aside. Pour half of the lemon juice into the breadcrumb mix along with 3 ¼ fl oz. iced water. Combine this all together to make more of a dough.

4) Pulse in the rest of the chilled butter, not over-doing it though, and ensure that there are still flecks of butter visible within the dough.

5) Roll the dough out into a large, thin rectangle. Fold the two ends to meet in the middle, and then in half again the other way too. Roll out again. Repeat this process 3 times, leaning at least 15 minutes between each roll and fold, chill the pastry for 30 minutes.

6) Melt the remaining butter in a pan. Then, add in the zest of the lemon, raisins, muscovado sugar, cinnamon, ginger, allspice, and the zest and half of the juice of the orange.

7) Preheat the oven to 390°F. Line a baking tray with greaseproof paper.

8) Roll the chilled pastry out to about 1 inch thick and cut into rounds, each one a little less than 5 inches across. You'll likely have enough dough for 8.

9) Spoon a heaped tablespoon of the filling into the centre of each round. Gather the outsides of the pastry around and squeeze together over the filling, closing up the gap. Try to make this as smooth as possible.

10) Use a rolling pin to flatten each round a little. The juice from the fruit should just being seeping out. Then, using a sharp knife, cut 2 slits in the top of each round.

11) Beat the egg. Lightly crush the sugar cubes so that you still have some lumps. Mix the sugar into the egg and brush over the Eccles cakes.

12) Bake for 15-20 minutes until golden brown and the fruit filling is beginning to seep out and become sticky.

Tips: Try to leave as much of the butter flecks in the pastry as possible, as this is what causes the delicious flakiness.

For a more warming treat, and to get a little fire in the belly, add some brandy or sherry to the fruit filling to taste.

Carrot & Walnut Cake

No longer just for rabbits, or a boring 'meat and two veg', carrot has burst its way into the sweet scene with recipes such as this one. Carrot cake is so deliciously moist due to the high water constant of the vegetables themselves that you really can't go far wrong with this cake!

Serves: 8

Preparation time: 60 minutes

Ingredients:

- 10 ½ oz. self-raising flour
- 8 ¾ oz. cream cheese
- 8 ½ fl oz. sunflower oil
- 8 oz. muscovado sugar
- 5 oz. peeled carrots
- 4 eggs
- 2 ½ oz. walnuts, plus extra to decorate
- 2 oz. raisins
- 2 teaspoons baking powder
- 1 teaspoon mixed spice
- 1 teaspoon ginger
- ¾ oz. icing sugar

Serving suggestion:

Nothing goes with carrot like orange. Treat yourself to a slice of this for breakfast on the weekend with a glass of freshly squeezed orange juice.

1) Preheat the oven to 350°F and line 2 equal-sized round cake tins with greaseproof paper.

2) Grate the carrots and chop the walnuts up small, leaving some extra for decoration.

3) Whisk together the sunflower oil, eggs and sugar. Once the mix has thickened, stir in the carrots, raisins, walnuts, baking powder, mixed spice and ginger.

4) Divide the mix evenly between the tins and bake for 35 minutes, or until springy to the touch but firm.

5) Whisk together the cream cheese and the icing sugar.

6) Trim the domed top off of one of the cakes and then top it with a layer of the cream cheese. Place the second cake on top and spread on the remaining cream cheese. Decorate with the remaining walnuts however you like.

Tips: Full-fat cream cheese will make a thicker icing. Low fat cream cheese may become too runny after whisking and may not stick so well.

A nice way to decorate is to just half the walnuts and place around the outside edge of the cake so that each slice will be topped with one.

Citrus Madeira Loaf

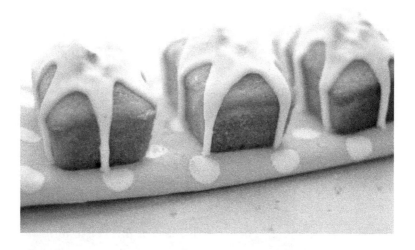

Probably the loaf cake of all loaf cakes is the timeless classic, Madeira. This loaf is flavored with orange and lemon to give it the citrus flavour that just goes so well with the close texture of this cake. This recipe even looks great too – topped with icing and candied peel.

Serves: 8

Preparation time: 80 minutes

Ingredients:

- 8 oz. caster sugar
- 7 oz. self-raising flour
- 5 ½ oz. butter
- 5 ¼ oz. icing sugar
- 4 eggs
- 3 oranges
- 2 unwaxed lemons
- Pinch of salt

Serving suggestion:

1) Preheat the oven to 350°F and line a loaf tin with greaseproof paper.

2) Beat the butter and 5 ½ oz. caster sugar together until light and fluffy. Beat in 2 of the eggs. Add the second 2 eggs one at a time with a tablespoon of flour each and beat the mixture well.

3) Sift the rest of the flour into the mix and add a pinch of salt. Stir well.

4) Grate the zest off of 2 of the oranges and 1 of the lemons and stir into the batter.

5) Pour the mix evenly into the loaf tin. Bake for 60 minutes until an inserted skewer comes out clean.

6) Meanwhile, dissolve the remaining caster sugar with 3 ¼ fl oz. of water in a saucepan. Once boiling, remove from the heat.

7) Take a vegetable peeler and peel off long strips of peel from the remaining orange and lemon. Stir the peel into the syrup. Return the pan to the heat and leave simmering on low for 5-7 minutes, until the peel is softened. Remove from the heat and allow to cool a little, before draining the liquid and allowing the peel to dry.

8) Juice an orange and a lemon. Add 1 tablespoon of juice from each to the icing sugar to make a runny icing. Add a little extra juice if necessary to thin it down even more.

9) Once the cake has cooled a little, drizzle the icing over the top and decorate with the candied peel.

Tips: We don't like wastage! So, don't fret about the leftover orange and lemon. You could make a zingy lemon curd or a little glass of fresh orange juice.

Keep the icing pretty runny to allow for a dripping look when decorating.

Apple Charlotte

No, this is not just a cute name suggestion for your daughter. This recipe is for apple Charlotte, a traditional English cake dating back to the mid-1800s. Apples are a-plenty in the English countryside, and so what better way to use them than in a delicious cake!

Serves: 6

Preparation time: 80 minutes

Ingredients:

- 8 oz. cooking apples
- 8 oz. sweet eating apples
- 8 slices white bread
- 7 ¼ oz. butter
- 3 ½ oz. brown sugar
- 3 ½ fl oz. double cream
- 1 oz. caster sugar
- 1 egg
- 1 teaspoon vanilla extract
- 1 teaspoon cinnamon
- 1 teaspoon nutmeg

Serving suggestion:

Sweet, sticky and caramel-y means that this delicious dessert could maybe do with something to cut through all the sugar. We suggest a glass of spiced rum or brandy.

1) Peel and chop all of the apples.

2) Melt 1 oz. of the butter in the saucepan and add the apples. Add the caster sugar, cinnamon, nutmeg, and vanilla extract and cook until the apples start breaking down into a purée.

3) Separate the egg and add the yolk into the apple, stirring well.

4) Cut the crusts off of the bread. Butter one side.

5) Line a pudding tin with as much of the bread as necessary. Allow the sides to overlap a little.

6) Spoon in the apple mixture and then top with the remaining bread.

7) Place a plate on top of the pudding and weigh it down with a can for an hour and preheat the oven to 400°F.

8) Cover the pudding with foil and bake for 30 minutes.

9) Meanwhile, melt together the remaining 3 ½ oz. of butter with the cream and brown sugar. Bring it to the boil and allow it to thicken for 5 minutes to become a dark sauce.

10) Remove the foil and spoon on the caramel sauce to cover the top of the pudding. Bake for a further 10 minutes.

11) Serve with the extra caramel sauce drizzled on top.

Tips: You could also serve this with ice cream or clotted cream to break through the sweetness.

Remember to taste the apple mix before baking, and add extra spice if you wish.

Rhubarb Crumble

Another of the many fruits available in Britain and not on some more exotic lands is the tart yet sweet rhubarb. When it's rhubarb season, you'd better pay attention and stock up because there are a whole load of delicious desserts to be made with these pink sticks. Here's a recipe for the Sunday afternoon classic, rhubarb crumble and custard.

Serves: 4

Preparation time: 70 minutes

Ingredients:

- 14 oz. rhubarb
- 10 fl oz. full-fat milk
- 6 ¼ oz. plain flour
- 4 egg yolks
- 3 ½ oz. butter
- 2 ¾ oz. caster sugar
- 2 ¼ oz. brown sugar
- 2 tablespoons corn flour
- 2 teaspoons vanilla extract
- Pinch of salt

Serving suggestion:

Yes, you can shop buy custard, but nothing is like homemade custard steaming, fresh from the pan over your baking hot rhubarb crumble. Bliss!

1) Preheat the oven to 400°F.

2) Chop the rhubarb into inch-long pieces.

3) Toss the rhubarb in the brown sugar, cornflour, and one teaspoon of vanilla extract.

4) Cube the butter and crumb together with 5 ¼ oz. of the plain flour.

5) Once the mixture resembles breadcrumbs, mix in 1 ¾ oz. of the caster sugar and a pinch of salt.

6) Place the rhubarb into a deep dish and then top with the crumb. Bake for 35-40 minutes, until golden brown and the juices are bubbling.

7) 15 minutes or so before the crumble is ready, you can make the custard. Separate the eggs. Into the yolks, whisk the remaining ounce of caster sugar and plain flour with a teaspoon of vanilla extract. Heat the milk on a low heat so that it's not quite boiling. Then, add the milk a little at a time to the yolk mix, whisking well after each addition. Return the mix to the heat and whisk for 10 minutes. Remove from the heat once thickened and continue to whisk for another minute or two.

Tips: Rhubarb often shrinks down when cooked, so pile a lot of filling in to avoid a disappointingly empty crumble at the end!

Ensure that you keep constantly whisking the custard to avoid it being lumpy.

Jam Roly Poly

It's time for another school dinner classic. For a start, the name is fun! Jam Roly Poly is a simple pastry mix rolled up with a sticky sweet jam filling. It's so easy to make that this is the perfect treat to try out with the kids.

Serves: 8

Preparation time: 70 minutes

Ingredients:

- 8 ¾ oz. self-raising flour
- 5 tablespoons raspberry jam
- 4 ½ oz. suet
- 1 cup fresh raspberries
- 1 egg
- ¾ oz. caster sugar
- ¾ fl oz. milk
- Pinch of salt
- Brown sugar for dusting

Serving suggestion:

Here is another fruity bake which would be complimented perfectly by some thick vanilla custard.

1) Preheat the oven to 400°F and line a deep baking tray with greaseproof paper.

2) Sieve the flour into a bowl with the sugar and a pinch of salt.

3) Grate the suet on top of the flour mix.

4) Stir the mix whilst adding the milk, a little splash at a time to bring everything together into a soft dough.

5) Roll the dough out into a large rectangle, about 1-2 inch thickness.

6) Evenly spread the jam, leaving a ½ inch border around the edges. Sprinkle in the fresh raspberries too.

7) Brush the edges with water, or a little extra milk if you have it.

8) Carefully but firmly roll up the dough from the short side.

9) Beat the egg and then paste it over the top to glaze. Sprinkle on a little brown sugar.

10) Transfer to the baking tin, ensuring that the sealed edge is down. Bake for 30-40 minutes until the dough is cooked through and golden.

Tips: Be careful when rolling out the dough to get the thickness correct. Too thick will make it very difficult to roll up and too thin will mean it's not sturdy enough to support being rolled.

Switch out the raspberries for other fruit if you like! Strawberry, blackberry or blueberry would be good.

Apple Pie

When the wind is blowing and the leaves are falling, really there's only one thing to do, and that is… curl up on the couch with a slice of steaming hot apple pie, whilst watching all the horrible weather going on outside. Wanna know how to make an apple pie just like Grandma? Read on.

Serves: 6

Preparation time: 50 minutes

Ingredients:

- 28 oz. Bramley apples
- 14 oz. plain flour
- 6 oz. butter
- 3 oz. brown sugar
- 3 oz. raisins

- 1 tablespoon caster sugar
- 1 tablespoon lemon juice
- ½ tablespoon cinnamon
- ½ tablespoon nutmeg
- Pinch of salt

Serving suggestion:

Here you have basically 3 options – vanilla ice cream, custard, or pouring cream. Oh, wait, there is the fourth option – all 3!

1) Preheat the oven to 400°F and lightly grease a pie dish.

2) Peel and core the apples, then chop them into thick slices. In a bowl, pour the lemon juice over them to prevent them from turning brown.

3) Into a bowl, sift the flour and add a pinch of salt. Crumb in the butter to create a breadcrumb mix and then also stir in the caster sugar.

4) Bring the mix together as a dough, adding in a little cold water if necessary to help bind.

5) Separate the dough into thirds. Combine two of the thirds and roll out to ½ in thickness. Use this dough to line the bottom of the pie dish. Allow a little extra to overhang the edges, an inch at most.

6) With the apples, mix the raisins with the cinnamon and nutmeg and most of the brown sugar.

7) Pour the apple mix into the pastry base.

8) Roll out the last third of pastry. Dampen the edges of the base and then layer the final part over the top.

9) Pinch the edges together and trim off any excess. Cut 3 slashes in the top of the pie, to allow the steak to escape.

10) Bake for 10 minutes before lowering the temperature to 375°F. Then, sprinkle the remaining brown sugar on top and bake for another 20-25 minutes until golden brown.

Tips: In many a photograph of a traditional English apple pie, you'll see a cute little leaf decoration on top. Take the excess pastry and fashion your own little leaves to sit on top in the centre of your pie.

This recipe specifies the use of Bramley apples. These cooking apples are denser and hold their structure much better than regular eating apples. If Bramleys aren't available, try to use the coolest type of cooking apple that you can, in order to get the correct texture.

Brandy Snaps

If you're unfamiliar, these are basically awesome little crunchy tubes, filled with whipped cream. These were a huge deal back in the day, but we say that we should still be eating and celebrating them now! Unfortunately, these don't contain any real brandy, so we've cheekily added some into the filling for you!

Makes: 16

Preparation time: 40 minutes

Ingredients:

- 5 fl oz. whipping cream
- 3 teaspoons brandy
- 2 oz. butter
- 2 oz. Demerara sugar
- 2 oz. golden syrup
- 1 ¾ oz. plain flour
- ½ teaspoon ginger
- ½ teaspoon lemon juice
- A little oil

Serving suggestion:

These are another little treat that look adorable as part of a delicate afternoon tea.

1) Preheat the oven to 350°F and line a baking tray with greaseproof paper.

2) Dress the handle of a wooden spoon with oil.

3) Melt together the butter, sugar and golden syrup. Leave it to cool a little and then stir in the flour and ginger.

4) Drop a tablespoon at a time into the baking tray. Leave plenty of room, as these spread a lot when cooking.

5) Bake for 8-10 minutes, until the discs are golden and have lace-like cracks.

6) After having been out of the oven for a minute or so, shape each snap into a cylinder by draping and wrapping it over the handle of the wooden spoon. Leave aside to continue to harden.

7) Whisk together the cream with the brandy to form stiff peaks. Then, pipe into the snaps.

Tips: Since these need shaping whilst still warm, it's often best to work in 2 or even 3 smaller batches, to avoid them cooking and becoming unworkable by the time you get to the last ones.

If at some point, they do get too cool to be pliable, you can simply return them to the oven for a minute or two to soften again.

Chocolate Bread and Butter Pudding

Bread and butter pudding is a truly British delight, dating back to wartime Britain. Food was on a ration, and very valuable, so nothing could be wasted. If your bread had gotten a little hard, no worries, you could bake it into something sweet and delicious. And, just to mix things up a bit, we've made this recipe a chocolate version.

Serves: 10

Preparation time: 40 minutes

Ingredients:

- 14 ¼ fl oz. whipping cream
- 10 slices of bread
- 5 ¼ oz. milk chocolate
- 3 eggs
- 2 ½ oz. caster sugar
- 2 ¼ oz. butter
- ¾ oz. cocoa powder

Serving suggestion:

For those chocoholics amongst us, a thick, homemade chocolate custard would be the perfect accompaniment to this pudding.

1) Lightly grease a large casserole dish and chop the bread to fit the dish, usually each slice should be cut in half. Line the bread up in the dish.

2) In a bowl over a pan of simmering water, melt the butter, chocolate, cream and sugar until smooth. Stir well and remove from the heat.

3) Whisk the eggs and add to the melted chocolate mixture. Then, pour this mix all over the bread, allowing it to reach to the bottom and cover everything.

4) Leave the dish to sit for an hour or two to allow as much of the sauce to absorb into the bread as possible.

5) 10 minutes before you're ready to start baking, preheat the oven to 350°F.

6) Bake for 30 minutes to create a crunchy top, but a soft and saucy inside.

Tips: You can switch out the regular bread for fruit bread if you wish, for some extra added sweetness, and probably some raisins!

This obviously lends itself to customising. Add in a sprinkle of raisins, dried orange, peanuts, marshmallows, or anything else your heart may desire!

West Country Scones

Down in the West Country, baking means one thing – scones! There's a little (!) rivalry though, surrounding these delicious afternoon treats. It's Devon vs Cornwall, cream first vs jam first. We don't wish to express an opinion either way, so try one of each and then pick your side!

Makes: 10

Preparation time: 35 minutes

Ingredients:

- 17 ½ oz. plain flour
- 10 tablespoons strawberry jam
- 10 tablespoons clotted cream
- 8 ½ fl oz. milk
- 3 ½ oz. caster sugar
- 3 ½ oz. butter
- 1 egg
- 1 teaspoon baking powder

Serving suggestion:

Make this into the perfect West Country experience and take yourself to some rugged countryside to enjoy these with a cup of tea.

1) Preheat the oven to 350°F and line a baking tray with greaseproof paper.

2) Sift together the flour, baking powder, and sugar.

3) Using your fingertips, rub in the butter. Then, add the milk and mix well into a dough.

4) Tun the dough out into a floured surface and knead well for 3-5 minutes.

5) Roll the dough to an inch thickness and cut into rounds, roughly 2 inches across.

6) Beat the egg and brush the wash across the top of the scones.

7) Bake for 15 minutes until well-risen and lightly browned.

8) Serve each with a tablespoon of clotted cream and a tablespoon of strawberry jam. As for which way round they go, the choice is yours!

Tips: The recipe calls for clotted cream. This is not the same as whipped cream. Whilst you could switch it out for whipped cream, clotted cream would be the most traditional way.

You can also add in a cup of raisins for added sweetness. Alternatively, cut out the sugar from the dough and add in cheese and onion to make savoury scones.

Mince Pies

A mince pie may not sound too appealing... if the idea coming to mind is ground up meat encased in dry pastry. Let me explain though, that British 'mincemeat' usually refers to a hearty, wintry mix of fruits and spices. Stick that inside some sweet, crumbly pastry and we've got ourselves a winner!

Makes: 36

Preparation time: 60 minutes + make ahead time for the mincemeat

Ingredients:

- 8 ¾ oz. plain flour
- 7 oz. dried cranberries
- 5 oz. raisins
- 2 ½ oz. brown sugar
- 2 oz. vegetable shortening
- 2 oz. butter
- 2 fl oz. port
- 2 tablespoons honey
- 1 clementine
- 1 teaspoon cinnamon
- 1 teaspoon ginger
- ¾ fl oz. brandy
- ½ cup fresh orange juice
- ½ teaspoon cloves
- ½ teaspoon almond extract
- ½ teaspoon vanilla extract
- Pinch of salt
- Icing sugar to dust

Serving suggestion:

Snuggle down for the evening in front of a roaring fire with a plate of these and a glass of something warming – we suggest sherry, port, or even a Bailey's!

1) We need to make the mincemeat in advance. It will keep for up to 2 weeks, so you can make it way beforehand. Over a low heat, dissolve the brown sugar in the port, stirring well. Zest and juice the clementine and add both into the mix. Also, stir in the cranberries, cinnamon, ginger, cloves, raisins, and brandy. Allow the mix to simmer for 20 minutes. Then, leave the mix to cool a little before stirring in the brandy, honey, and almond and vanilla extracts. Squish the mix a little with the back of a spoon.

2) Now, onto the pastry. The quantity of 36 for this recipe is based on using a miniature muffin tin to bake these in. If you use a slightly bigger one, you'll just yield fewer pies. Sift the flour into a bowl and dollop the vegetable shortening in, a tablespoon at a time.

3) Dice the butter up small and add this into the bowl. Give the mixture just a stir or 2 to cover the butter in the flour. Then, cover with cling wrap and freeze for 20 minutes.

4) Combine the orange juice with a pinch of salt.

5) Then, blitz the flour mix into breadcrumbs. Add the orange juice little by little, starting to combine the dough. Once it's about the combine well, stop adding juice.

6) Knead the dough a little to form it together and then cling wrap the ball and chill it for 20 minutes.

7) Preheat the oven to 425°F. Grease the muffin tin.

8) Roll the dough out to really as thin as you can get it without it tearing. Then, use a cutter for the size of your tins to cut out discs. Leave between 1/3 and ¼ of the pastry.

9) Place the discs into the muffin tins, pressing them into the shape. Drop a teaspoon of mincemeat into the miniature size. For larger sizes, fill about 2/3 of the case with the mix.

10) To top the pies, cut stars out of the remaining dough and place one on top of each pie.

11) Bake for 10-15 minutes until lightly browned and then dust with icing sugar to serve.

Tips: If you need extra liquid when making your dough, use a little iced water.

To really go for a festive, wintry feel, serve these also with a brandy clotted cream or something similar.

Malt Loaf

It's hard to put a finger on just what it is that makes malt loaf so more-ish and quintessentially British. My guess is that incredible stickiness, even when the loaf is no longer fresh. Put your feet up with a slice or three of this delicious bake and relax.

Makes: 2 loaves

Preparation time: 60 minutes

Ingredients:

- 10 ½ oz. mixed dried fruit
- 8 ¾ oz. plain flour
- 5 ¼ oz. malt extract
- 5 fl oz. freshly brewed black tea
- 3 oz. muscovado sugar
- 2 eggs
- 1 teaspoon baking powder
- ½ teaspoon bicarbonate of soda

Serving suggestion:

The definitive way to eat malt loaf is sliced and slathered in butter.

1) Preheat oven to 300°F and line 2 loaf tins with greaseproof paper.

2) Into a mixing bowl, pour the hot tea. Stir in the dried fruit, the malt, and sugar.

3) Then, stir in the eggs.

4) Sift in the flour and also add the baking powder and then bicarbonate of soda. Stir well.

5) Pour the mixture into the loaf tins, and bake for 50 minutes.

Tips: This will actually get sticker as time goes on, so if you have self-control, wait a day or 2 before eating.

You can use a little extra malt extract as a glaze on top after baking, if you wish.

Treacle Tart

Here is a super simple treacle tart recipe that can be dressed up or down for any occasion! As long as you're looking to bring a whole load of sweetness and a wave of nostalgia, then this is the dessert for you!

Serves: 6

Preparation time: 90 minutes

Ingredients:

- 15 ¾ oz. golden syrup
- 9 oz. plain flour
- 6 ½ oz. butter
- 4 ¼ oz. brown bread
- 4 eggs
- 3 ½ oz. caster sugar
- 3 tablespoons double cream
- 1 oz. ground almonds
- Pinch of salt

Serving suggestion:

To cut through all the sugary sweetness of the tart, you could serve with raspberries dressed in lemon juice and a little pepper, and with some whipped cream.

1) Preheat oven to 350°F and grease a tart dish.

2) Mix together the flour, sugar and ground almonds and then rub in 4 ½ oz. of the butter to create a breadcrumb consistency.

3) Mix in 2 eggs. Then, cling wrap and chill for 30 minutes.

4) Roll the pastry out to about ¼ inch thickness and then line the tart dish with it, trimming the edges. Cover with greaseproof paper and fill with baking beans or dry rice.

5) Bake for 20 minutes until the pastry is turning golden brown.

6) Meanwhile, for the filling, melt the remaining butter in a pan until it browns. Then, pass it through a sieve.

7) Separate an egg and add into the butter the yolk, as well as the one last whole egg. Add in also the cream and a pinch of salt.

8) Blitz up the bread to make fine breadcrumbs.

9) Over the heat, stir the golden syrup and breadcrumbs, stirring well. Add this into the butter and cream mixture and stir so that everything is well combined. Then, pour this mix in to fill up the tart case.

10) Reduce the oven temperature to 280°F and bake for a further 20 minutes.

Tips: When rolling out the dough, although we want it thin, take care that it's not so thin that it starts to come apart, as this will only likely get worse during the baking process.

Some recipes use a pastry lattice over the top of the tart too. If you find yourself with extra pastry, why not give this a go?

Dense Dark Fruit Cake

If you were ever fortunate enough to have a British Grandma (they're great – always baking sweet treats and will usually give you candy and spoil you rotten!), then you will have fond memories of a rich, dense, heavy, dark fruit cake from her kitchen. Our recipe won't be filled with half the amount of love and experience that goes into Grandma's, but our dark fruit cake is pretty close.

Serves: 25

Preparation time: 180 minutes

Ingredients:

- 18 oz. currants
- 8 oz. glacé cherries
- 8 oz. candied citrus peel
- 8 oz. pecans
- 6 oz. dried prunes
- 6 oz. dried dates
- 6 oz. golden currants
- 4 fl oz. dark rum
- 3 eggs
- 3 tablespoons cocoa
- 2 oranges
- 2 teaspoons allspice
- 2 teaspoons cinnamon
- 2 teaspoons ginger
- 2 teaspoons nutmeg
- 1 ½ cups plain flour
- 1 teaspoon cloves
- 1 cup brown sugar
- ¾ cup butter
- ¾ cup molasses
- ½ cup ground almonds
- ½ cup sherry
- ½ teaspoon baking powder
- ½ teaspoon bicarbonate of soda

Serving suggestion:

As you will notice, this is a monster of a cake! Whip it up maybe at the start of a holiday, and don't let a visitor leave tour house without a slice!

1) Juice and zest the oranges.

2) In a pan over a medium heat, melt the butter. Then, add the orange juice and zest, both types of currant, dates, prunes, sugar, molasses, cinnamon, ginger, allspice, cloves, nutmeg, and sherry. Stir well and allow to simmer for 10 minutes.

3) Once this mix has cooled, beat in the eggs.

4) Sift together the flour, cocoa powder, ground almonds, baking powder, and bicarbonate of soda.

5) Fold the flour mix into the wet ingredients.

6) Chop the pecans and halve the glacé cherries. Then, stir these in, along with the candied citrus peel.

7) Heat the oven to 300°F and grease a large cake tin.

8) Pour the batter evenly into the tin.

9) Bake for at least 1 ½ hours, although it may take up to 2, depending on your tin size and oven. When done, the cake will be firm but still springy to the touch.

10) Use a fork to poke small holes all over the surface of the cake and gradually pour the rum over the top, allowing it all to soak in.

Tips: There is plenty of room for decoration with this cake. Keeping it traditional, marzipan would be a great additional on top, or even just some extra glacé cherries or nuts on top would work.

Another way of infusing the rum would be to soak some cheesecloth in it and then wrap the cake in the cloth, leaving it for at least 24 hours in a cool, dry place.

Scottish Shortbread

Let's take a wee trip up to bonny Scotland! This is the land of tartan, haggis and the Highland Games. Oh, and one more thing – shortbread. Traditional Scottish shortbread biscuits are crumbly, all-butter affairs, absolutely perfect for dunking in your tea.

Makes: 24

Preparation time: 35 minutes

Ingredients:

- 2 ½ cups plain flour
- 1 cup butter
- ½ cup brown sugar
- White sugar for dusting

Serving suggestion:

The sturdy texture of this shortbread makes it perfect for dunking! A steaming hot cup of tea would be good, or why not go all-Scottish and try it with a glass of Scotch whiskey, on the rocks.

1) Preheat the oven to 325°F.

2) Cream together the butter and sugar until light and fluffy.

3) Add in the flour and mix well.

4) Turn the dough out and knead for about 5 minutes.

5) Roll the dough out to ½ inch thickness and then cut into even strips, 1 inch by 3 inches. Prick the tops with a fork.

6) Spread evenly on a baking tray and bake for 20 minutes, until golden.

7) Dust with sugar to serve.

Tips: Shortbread lasts for weeks (unless eaten!) and makes a great gift, so why not up the quantities and make a larger batch at a time?

If you're really feeling like treating yourself, add some chocolate chips into the dough!

Victoria Sponge Cake

Introducing possibly the quintessential English bake to end them all – Victoria sponge cake! Delicious and regal, and named after Queen Victoria herself, this cake is a true crowd-pleaser.

Serves: 10

Preparation time: 90 minutes

Ingredients:

- 10 ½ oz. butter
- 7 oz. caster sugar
- 7 oz. self-raising flour
- 5 ½ oz. strawberry jam
- 5 oz. icing sugar, plus extra for dusting
- 4 eggs
- 2 tablespoons milk
- 1 teaspoon baking powder
- ½ teaspoon vanilla extract

Serving suggestion:

No proper English cake would be complete without a proper cup of English tea. Why not keep the Royal theme going and upgrade your traditional tea to an Early Grey or an Assam?

1) Preheat the oven to 375°F and line 2 equally-sized sandwich tins with greaseproof paper.

2) Beat together 7oz of the butter along with the caster sugar, flour, eggs, milk and baking powder to create a smooth batter.

3) Divide the mixture evenly between the 2 tins and try to make the top as smooth as possible by using a spatula.

4) Bake for 20 minutes, until a skewer can be inserted and come out clean and the top is firm and yet springy.

5) To make the buttercream icing for the filling, beat the remaining butter until smooth. Then, stir in the icing sugar and vanilla extract.

6) If the cakes have domed, trim the dome off of one layer, which will become the bottom. You should probably eat the trimmings, just to check that the cake went well! Then, spread the buttercream icing on the top of this layer.

7) Spread the jam over the buttercream and sandwich the second cake layer on top. Dust with a little extra icing sugar and enjoy!

Tips: If buttercream is too much effort, you can simply use whipped cream, but this won't stay sturdy for as long.

Be careful not to overcook the cake, as one of its crowning glories is how moist it is.

About the Author

Martha is a chef and a cookbook author. She has had a love of all things culinary since she was old enough to help in the kitchen, and hasn't wanted to leave the kitchen since. She was born and raised in Illinois, and grew up on a farm, where she acquired her love for fresh, delicious foods. She learned many of her culinary abilities from her mother; most importantly, the need to cook with fresh, homegrown ingredients if at all possible, and how to create an amazing recipe that everyone wants. This gave her the perfect way to share her skill with the world; writing cookbooks to spread the message that fresh, healthy food really can, and does, taste delicious. Now that she is a mother, it is more important than ever to make sure that healthy food is available to the next generation. She hopes to become a household name in cookbooks for her delicious recipes, and healthy outlook.

Martha is now living in California with her high school sweetheart, and now husband, John, as well as their infant daughter Isabel, and two dogs; Daisy and Sandy. She is a stay at home mom, who is very much looking forward to expanding their family in the next few years to give their daughter some siblings. She enjoys cooking with, and for, her family and friends, and is waiting impatiently for the day she can start cooking with her daughter.

Author's Afterthoughts

Thanks ever so much to each of my cherished readers for investing the time to read this book!

I know you could have picked from many other books but you chose this one. So, a big thanks for downloading this book and reading all the way to the end.

*Amazon gives newer Kindle device readers the opportunity to rate this book and share your thoughts via an **"automatic feed to your Facebook and Twitter accounts"**. I'd honored and grateful if you Scroll down to the last page to use the automated links with Facebook and Twitter if you are reading in a Kindle Reader.*

Thanks!

Martha Stephenson

CPSIA information can be obtained
at www.ICGtesting.com
Printed in the USA
BVHW031224151218
535691BV00001BA/83/P

9 781546 416968